BLACK LEGACY PRESS™

WWW.BLACKLEGACYPRESS.ORG

Putting the Most into Life

by
Booker T. Washington

Copyright © 2023 by BLP PUBLISHING

BLP PUBLISHING
Eastchester New York

For wholesale please visit:
www.BBWLogistics.com

Available wherever books are sold.

ISBN: 978-1-63652-139-8

PUTTING THE MOST INTO LIFE

by

BOOKER T. WASHINGTON

The chapters in this little book were originally part of a series of Sunday Evening Talks given by the Principal to the students of the Tuskegee Normal and Industrial Institute. They have been recast from the second to the third person, and many local allusions have been cut out. They are now sent out, in response to repeated requests, to a larger audience than that to which they were first spoken.

BOOKER T. WASHINGTON

Tuskegee Institute, Alabama
August 10, 1906

CONTENTS

CHAPTER I

Health a Requisite for Effective Living

H E individual who puts the most into life is the one who gets the most out of life. The first requisite for making life effective for one's self or society is a sound body. There have been many people who in spite of weak bodies have enriched the world by noble thought and work. There has been a long line of physically weak men who have helped the world onward; but the rule holds that the best work has been done by men and women of vigorous health.

It is important that the Negro race in its present condition shall learn just as quickly as possible how to have good, strong, healthy working bodies, for so much is dependent upon them. In the world of industry, the world of commerce, all mental activity and spiritual endeavor,—no matter in what direction one's attention or energies may be turned, strong bodies are needed to meet the demand. There are a few simple rules which should serve as guide-posts to those who would make the most of their physical being. One of the conditions of a good, strong, working body is contact with fresh air. In the early days of this school, when we were housed in shacks and cabins, whatever else we lacked, we were, by virtue of necessity, abundantly supplied with air; but now that we are getting into plastered buildings, with good floors and windows and doors, there is danger of suffering from poorly ventilated rooms and a lack of health-giving air.

Those who live in the large cities would do well to become disciples of Wordsworth, and with him learn to know the inspiration and strength that come from wood and forest,—the joy of intimate acquaintance with birds and flowers. The individual who has the privilege of living on the farm, and coming in contact with the earth and grass and trees and real things, is the individual who, provided he has an eye to see and an ear to hear, is most to be envied.

Next in importance to an abundance of fresh air is the habit of regular, systematic exercise. People often think that this kind of exercise costs a great deal of money, that it means costly apparatus and artificial fixtures. Not so. It requires no great outlay of time or energy for the boy on the farm to breathe deeply as he follows the plough or scatters the seeds. And yet, simple exercises of this kind are essential to the life of a race whose mortality from pulmonary diseases is alarming. Every boy in the machine shop knows how necessary it is to keep his machinery well oiled and in good running condition. Then, too, every such boy knows the importance of keeping every part of his machinery as clean as possible. Now, your body is a machine, but how much more delicate and intricate than any made by man! how much more necessary to keep it in good running condition and absolutely clean in order that it may do its best work!

In addition to pure air and cleanliness, I want to speak of the wearing of comfortable clothing as another essential to right living. I am glad to see that the world is fast getting away from the old habits that used to enslave people in this matter of dressing—the habit exercised by many of wearing small shoes, for instance, until their feet were cramped in severe pains merely to have the world think they had small feet. What does it matter to the world whether a person has small feet or large feet? Who ever stops to think whether great poets, historians, the great workers in economic and religious life,—men and women who have really accomplished something,—had large or small feet, whether they wore fours or eights, or wore large or small corsets or none. I am glad to see that all peoples and races are getting away from that kind of thing, and I want the Tuskegee students to make up their minds to buy shoes to fit no matter what the number. We consider the Chinese ridiculous to keep their feet cruelly cramped in order that they may be small, but many of us in somewhat less degree are guilty of the same thing.

The importance of temperance has been repeated over and over again from this platform; and intemperance in eating or sleeping is not less disgusting than intemperance in drink.

The world's work is to be done by men and women of vigorous intellect; but the sound mind must have its foundation in a body which is kept clean and made comfortable by proper clothing, pure air, regular exercise and wholesome food. No workman, however competent, can do good work unless his tools are kept in proper repair. My plea is that the young Negro students shall acquire strong working bodies to be used as tools to serve therewith their fellows and their Maker. This is the end of all living.

Booker T. Washington

CHAPTER II

Some of the Qualities Essential to the Most Successful School Life

HE student who would put the most into his school life must first of all be happy. I do not believe it is possible for a student to accomplish very much, certainly not the most, while he is in school, unless he learns to be happy in all his relations in school life. If the students are unhappy there is something wrong with the institution, or with the teachers, or with the student body. The normal state of a student in a well-ordered institution is a happy one. It is impossible to get the most out of the life of any institution unless there is joy in working out the ideals of the institution. The student should make himself familiar with the purposes of the school to which he seeks admission, and having made the choice, he should be loyal to its traditions and purposes.

The Bible teaches over and over again that freedom, without which happiness is impossible, is self-imposed restraint, that to be really free we must live within the law. He who lives outside the law is a slave. The freeman is the man who lives within the law, whether that law be the physical or the divine. All life is governed by law, and the student must acquire freedom by obedience to law. The students in any institution are divided into two classes: the happy, contented, ambitious, hopeful ones, who have faith in the institution and respect for its traditions, and the miserable, discontented, grumbling class. One class live not only within the letter but in the spirit of the law, and are consequently happy. The second class are miserable, discontented and hopeless because they try to live outside the law. No student can get much out of any institution who does not enter whole-heartedly into its spirit, its traditions and its ideals.

The ability to do hard methodical work is one of the prizes which every school worthy of the name offers to its students. The years at school not infrequently give bent to the whole life. The student who does slipshod work at school is more than likely to lack direction in his subsequent career. But mental strength comes not as a bequest. It is a prize that must be contended for right earnestly, and dictionary, cyclopaedia, text-book and shop are tools which instructors place in the hands of students to help them win the prize. The proper use of these tools must depend finally upon the individual student. No one gets much out of life who does not make his education a real, vital part of himself. Many people have education very much as a parrot has at his command a certain number of words or sentences. The words and sentences that the parrot utters are no real part of him. They are merely something tacked on to the parrot, and foreign to his real natural make-up. Some people use education as they use their "Sunday clothes," on extra occasions only. They bring their education into play when they are in the company of others, commit a few quotations and use big words which have no working place in their vocabulary. To try to make education a real part of one's self is the way to get most out of one's school life. Just as the food a man eats becomes a part of his blood and bone, so should education become a vital part of him. Education must be digested and assimilated in order to make it significant.

The student who leaves undone immediate duties because of bodily laziness is leaving happiness far behind him. Sins of commission and sins of omission alike tend to weakness. Our ability to make the world better depends entirely upon our ability to use every opportunity to make ourselves better. A largeness of life, a variety of interests and breadth of view are among the prizes which a school offers to its students. These qualities the ignorant man does not possess. Largeness of life and breadth of vision give faith in the future; that largeness makes one person take the long view when the other is taking the short view; that largeness lifts the educated person far above the temptation to gossip about little things, above the temptation to get down into the mud and slime with which weaker individuals are smeared.

To be loyal and obedient to the legislation of an institution, to make thrifty use of text-book and shop and farm and every part of the school equipment, is to attain that mental strength that makes for largeness of life and breadth of view. These qualities come not by observation, but they do come by conscientious work in season and out of season. They are all within the reach of the student who is willing to work for them, and they are all essential to real happiness.

Booker T. Washington

CHAPTER III

A Word to Prospective Teachers about Putting the Most into their Work

T

HE large problem of the teacher is not to impart knowledge and maintain discipline. The larger problem is to bring school life and real life into closer contact. With the average teacher, as with the average student, there is very little connection between the school and life as it is actually lived every day outside the school-room; and as long as this is true there will be ground for reasonable and just criticism.

In the primary school, the intermediary school and the high school there is often little, if any, connection between life as it is lived in the shop, on the farm, in business and in the home. It cannot but prove of mutual advantage if the teacher can bring school life into actual touch with the life of the people about him. The interest of the parents will be increased just in proportion as they find that the teacher is making his instruction stimulate and vitalize conditions outside the school-room.

It is difficult for the parent of the country child to note the results of education through the usual processes and channels of knowledge. Colored parents depend upon seeing the results of education in ways not true of the white parent. It is important then that the colored teacher in this generation should give special attention to bringing school life into closer touch with real life. Any education is to my mind "high" which enables the individual to do the very best work for the people by whom he is surrounded. Any education is "low" that does not make for character and effective service.

The average teacher in the public schools is very likely to yield to the temptation of thinking that he is educating an individual when he is teaching him to reason out examples in Arithmetic, to prove propositions in Geometry and to recite pages of History. He conceives this to be the end of education. Herein is the sad deficiency in many teachers who are not able to use History, Arithmetic, Geometry as means to an end. They get the idea that the student who has mastered a certain number of pages in a text-book is educated, forgetting that text-books are at best but tools, and in many cases ineffective tools, for the development of man. Modern educators are getting more and more away from books. Now this will be hard for the average teacher who has worked out all the problems in Arithmetic and proved them by the answers in the book, but I believe that the best educational thought tends toward the study of real things and not mere books.

One of the ways of bringing the school into closer touch with society is to make school surroundings, including the grounds and buildings, as homelike and as attractive as possible. The school-rooms are in too many cases cold and barren. In schools of this sort there is little connection between the home and the school. I believe that the teacher should study the home surroundings of his pupils and become more intimately acquainted with the parents. When teachers are able to make their school-rooms inviting and are able to project their influence into the home life of the pupils, there will be few absentees or truants. A child cannot be expected to leave a comfortable, attractive and convenient home to go into a dull, inconvenient, uncomfortable school-room, nor can it be expected that pupils will leave comfortable chairs at home and go into school-rooms where they must sit on stools with their feet six or eight inches from the floor.

It is hardly necessary to say that the teacher should set the example for the student in the matter of cleanliness and neatness. The teacher who would preach against grease spots, rents in clothes and buttonless jackets must see to it that he is himself without fault in these respects. When I go into a school and notice that the instructor has buttons off his coat, I am at once convinced that he is not the right teacher. I do not believe that there is much that the student can learn at that school that can be put into practice in real life. I believe that the teacher should not only set an example himself, but that he should go further than this: he should see that every boy and girl in his school is familiar with the practical applications of soap and water, and knows the work of the tooth-brush and the darning-needle. Some parents may at first resent this encroachment upon their special domain, but persistence in an endeavor of this sort will finally cause the parents to look upon the teacher as a new force in the community. The average parent cannot appreciate how many examples Johnny has worked that day, how many questions in History he has answered; but when he says, "Mother, I cannot go back to that school until all the buttons are sewed on my coat," the parent will at once become conscious of school influence in the home. This will be the best kind of advertisement. The button propaganda tends to make the teacher a power in the community. A few lessons in applied Chemistry will not be amiss. Take grease spots, for example. The teacher who with tact can teach his pupils to keep even threadbare clothes neatly brushed and free from grease spots is extending the school influence into the home and is adding immeasurably to the self-respect of the home.

In the school-houses in the city, and in many of the larger towns and country districts, janitors do all the work of cleaning. This may be necessary in city schools, where it is not possible for the children to do all the work of beautifying and cleaning the school building, but when all this work is done by outsiders the children are robbed of part of their instruction and they thus lose a very important lesson in cleanliness and order which it is the duty of the teacher to give. Think of the time lost in the average family looking for the broom when the time comes to sweep the floor. At this time all business suspends. Mother cries out first, "Where is the broom?" The older sister cries to John and Susie and Jane, "Where is the broom?" and that kind of thing goes on every day in the week and year. It takes the average family from ten to twelve minutes every day to find the broom. Now, we should teach a different lesson in our schools. We can teach in the first place that there are two ways for the broom to be put up, a proper and an improper way. We can teach the children that there is a place for the dust-pan and the dust-cloth and the match-box. The match-box is another thing that suspends business. Every night when the matches are wanted, everything goes helter-skelter. This is a larger problem than the broom, there being absolutely no light on the subject. The children should be taught that there must be a definite place for the broom and for the match-box, and it is surprising how quickly these lessons will be taken from the school-room into the home. Even the listless parents will be roused to interest by such practical teaching. The child who goes to school in a room that is clean and attractive will not long be content to live in a home that is dirty and disorderly.

I was recently in a school-room in South Carolina. The teacher had a reputation for being a well-fitted instructor, and I expected much of him. He was teaching the children by the latest methods. The children sang well, they recited their lessons well, but the fact that one third of the plastering was missing made the greatest impression on me. I could not detect the slightest attempt on the part of the teacher or students to see that the plastering was restored. I should have suspended school a day or two until the plastering could be replaced, rather than teach day after day by silent approval a lesson of disorder. If the teacher is careless, the pupils will accept his standards and go through life in an indifferent, slipshod manner. If from the first day they enter school they are surrounded with object lessons of order and cleanliness, more will have been done to educate them in a large and helpful way than if they had centred their interest in books alone.

Order and beauty are sacrificed in many of our schools because one third or one fourth of the window-glass is out. Sometimes I have seen obsolete hats and discarded dresses doing duty in the absence of window-glass or window-panes knocked out in order that the stovepipe might be run through the broken place. The child never outlives the impression made by such a sight. The parents will join their children in helping to patch broken plastering if the teacher will take the lead. When the plastering is mended, a few pictures should be placed on the walls, and in this work the parents' coöperation can be depended upon. Teachers must put not less conscience but more thought into the work for the children to whose lives they are giving direction. By putting into their work more of their better selves, more of their personality, teachers will add not only to their own happiness and usefulness, but will be doing real work toward hastening the coming of that kingdom for which they daily pray.

Booker T. Washington

CHAPTER IV

Industrial Efficiency an Aid to The Higher Life

T was Emerson who said that "One generation clears the forests, the next builds the palaces." Each generation is very anxious to engage in the building of the palaces, an ambition which is altogether laudable, but the forests must first be cleared or there will be no palaces. And so it falls to the lot of every successful individual of every race and nation to engage at some time or period in their existence in dealing in a large degree with the industrial or material affairs of life.

The forms of industry that occupy the majority of people in a civilized country may be classed under one of the following heads: first and perhaps most largely, the production of raw material in one form or another; the second step is the manufacturing of these materials; third, the problem of transportation and getting these products on the markets of the world, and having them properly distributed and economically and wisely consumed.

The production of cotton in the South presents a familiar example of all these processes. The growing of cotton is an industry largely in the hands of my race; in the second step, the manufacturing of cotton, the colored people have as yet little part; in putting these materials on the market through the medium of steamboats, steam-cars, and their distribution through wholesale and retail establishments, colored people have diminishing interests. The lesson for all young people to learn in this busy industrial age is to deal with materials, whether at first hand in getting something out of the soil, or as constructing or distributing agents, so as to increase the value of the material they handle and to make themselves more useful as individuals.

The main source of all productiveness is in the soil, and the work of getting out of the soil all that can be gotten out of it has, in recent years, made agriculture an intellectual pursuit. It is very important to note the progress of the world during the last few years, when people have learned to put more into life by putting brains and skill and confidence into all industrial operations. A few years ago the man who was going to be a farmer made almost no preparation for his work. Skill and intelligence were not considered necessary, but to-day in every civilized country there are institutions that have for their sole purpose the teaching of methods of getting everything possible out of the soil. A few years ago the mining of coal, copper, silver and gold was left to the most unintelligent, ignorant and unskilled people; there was little thought or skill put into preparation for this kind of work. To-day mining schools have been established in all important mining districts, and this industry has been so dignified that intelligent and skilful men delight to enter it. The same thing is true of forestry. Within the last few months a chair of Forestry has been established at Cornell University, where young men can learn all about the selection and cultivation of trees. The Department of Agriculture at Washington is spending over two million dollars yearly in showing people how to take care of the forests. The world is making all the material products serve not as masters but as servants, and servants in the sense that they are making people put more thought, more effort, more skill into life, and enabling them thus to get more abundant returns wherewith to enlarge and ennoble their lives. There are opportunities about us on every hand. The Southern farm offers great opportunities to every young man who will use his talents. The idea that farming means ploughing with one mule or digging the ground with a spade is fast disappearing, for this industry is developing into a high and dignified calling. Young women of maturer races than ours are making large economic successes in the raising of chickens, in fruit growing, in raising small berries; and young colored women should begin to get some of the benefits of these industries.

But the chance for material success in connection with industrial life is relatively of less importance than is the chance for the individual to get development through the mastering of difficulties in the management of industrial operations. The mere mastering of these difficulties has made many of the Captains of Industry of this country. Poverty discourages many a youth who starts out in the busy industrial world, but the fact that others have conquered poverty is an earnest that others, for centuries to come, will get courage and strength out of adverse struggle. The colored man starts out, it is true, with an additional handicap, but here is the chance for Negro youth to learn to turn disadvantages to advantages. A colored man born in poverty and an ex-slave owns to-day one of the largest tailoring establishments in one of the most prominent streets in the city of Boston. This man had learned the sweet uses of adversity and knew how to lay hold of disadvantages. His establishment is patronized by people who buy from him not in spite of the fact that he is a Negro, but because he is a Negro. The world needs men, be they white or black, who can rise on successive failures to useful citizenship. No person can enter industrial life without for a time feeling some days of almost complete failure, but mistakes and weariness beget confidence and experience.

All industrial operations and material progress should be used not as ends but as means of making life more comfortable, more useful and more beautiful. The intelligent farmer as he plants and works and harvests the cotton must remember that the production of cotton is not the end of his effort. Every bale of cotton can be turned into books, into opportunities for travel and study. The man who grows corn must remember that the growing of corn is not the end of life, but that the corn can be turned into refinements and beauties of a civilized life and a Christian home.

No one can doubt that the people who have built the railroads and constructed the great steamships that bind country to country have added to the wealth and happiness of the world. Finally, it must be remembered that the mastering of difficulties should bring poise, purpose and vision. I want every Tuskegee student as he finds his place in the surging industrial life about him to give heed to the things which are "honest and just and pure and of good report," for these things make for character, which is the only thing worth fighting for, either in this life or the next.

CHAPTER V

Making Religion A Vital Part of Living

DUCATED men and women, especially those who are in college or other institutions of learning, very often get the idea that religion is fit only for the common people and beneath the interest and sympathy of the educated man. In too many cases they are disposed to think that religion is for the weak, and that to express doubts concerning religion and the future life is an indication of a vigorous, independent mind. No young man or woman can make a greater error than this.

Some years ago, when I was in New York City, I went down to Wall Street to consult a friend as to methods of arranging for a large meeting. I wanted in this meeting to get interest centred in the work we are trying to do at Tuskegee. My friend said: "If you can secure the coöperation of four men in New York City, the success of your meeting will be assured." I went to the four men whose names had been given me and secured their interest and coöperation. Some weeks later there was a large meeting held in New York in the interest of the Young Men's Christian Association movement. In looking over the list of persons who were sponsors for this meeting I found the names of the four men whom my Wall Street friend had mentioned. He gave me these names, however, with no thought that they were leaders in the religious activity of New York City. He named them chiefly because he knew their standing in the commercial and business life of the city was secure, and that anything they said would attract the attention of the public and would secure the confidence of the people whose interest and aid we were seeking. And so it appears that the four men who at that time represented the commercial and business interest of New York were men who were closely identified with the religious life of the city, and were active in Sunday-school and church work, and connected with many other agencies which had to do with the uplifting of the masses. My observation has taught me that the people who stand for the most in the educational and commercial world and in the uplifting of the people are in some real way connected with the religious life of the people among whom they reside.

This being true we ought to make the most of our religious life and to avail ourselves of certain outward helps, helps which are not ends but aids to higher spiritual living. First the habit of regular attendance at some religious service should be cultivated. This is one of the outward helps toward inward grace. Nothing is ever lost by this habit of systematic devotion. But one says, "What good is accomplished by attending church?" Another says, "I stay away from religious service and I am just as good as those who go." To put the question another way, Was any one ever injured by regular attendance upon religious services? The man who allows himself to grow careless about sacred things yields to a temptation which is sure to drag him down. As you value your spiritual life, see to it that you do not lose the spirit of reverence for the Most High as revealed in your own life and experience, reverence for the Most High as revealed in the men and women about you, in the opening flower, the setting sun, and the song of the bird. Do not mistake denominationalism for reverence and religion. Religion is life, denominationalism is an aid to life.

Systematic reading and prayerful study of the Bible is the second outward help which I would commend to those whom I wish to see make the most of their spiritual life. Many people regard the Bible as a wonderful piece of literature only. The reading of the Bible as literature only brings its reward in that it throws new light on secular history and gives acquaintance with men and women and ideals which have been the inspiration of the noblest things that have ever been spoken or written. Nowhere in all literature can be found a finer bit of oratory than St. Paul's defence before King Agrippa. But praiseworthy as this kind of study is, I do not believe it is sufficient. The Bible should be read as a daily guide to right living and as a daily incentive to positive Christian service.

I think that no man who lives a merely negative religious life can ever know real spiritual joy. There are many people who pride themselves on the things they do not do. The negative Christian always suggests a lamp-post to me. The negative Christian says he is going to heaven because he does not lie. Neither does the lamp-post. The negative Christian does not steal. Neither does the lamp-post steal. He does not cheat, he does nothing of which he is ashamed: he is therefore blameless. The lamp-post has never done any one of these things. I do not want the Tuskegee students to be lamp-posts in their religious life, but I want them to turn their beliefs into energy that shall work into every detail of their lives.

Not less repulsive to me than the negative Christian is the one who is always using his religion as a means of escape from something, from hell fire or brimstone or some less remote punishment. This class of Christians use religion as people use the conjurer's bag or a disinfectant to ward off evil. They are not drawn to any vital thing in religion; they simply use it as a cloak to shield them from harm.

To live the real religious life is in some measure to share the character of God. The word "atonement," which occurs in the Bible again and again, means literally at-one-ment. To be at one with God is to be like God. Our real religious striving, then, should be to become one with God, sharing with Him in our poor human way His qualities and attributes. To do this, we must get the inner life, the heart right, and we shall then become strong where we have been weak, wise where we have been foolish. We are often criticised as a race because people say that our religion is not real. They say that our religion is superficial, that in spite of our attendance at religious services and protestations of faith we are guilty of petty pilfering, stealing, lying and of walking crookedly in many directions. Whenever this criticism is true it means that we have not learned what the religious life really means. We must learn to incorporate God's laws into our thoughts and words and acts. Frequent reference is made in the Bible to the freedom that comes from being a Christian. A man is free just in proportion as he learns to live within God's laws, and he makes grievous mistakes and serious blunders the minute he departs from these laws.

As a race we are inclined, I fear, to make too much of the day of judgment. We have the idea that in some far-off period there is going to be a great and final day of judgment, when every individual will be called up, and all his bad deeds will be read out before him and all his good deeds made known. I believe that every day is a day of judgment, that we reap our rewards daily, and that whenever we sin we are punished by mental and physical anxiety and by a weakened character that separates us from God. Every day is, I take it, a day of judgment, and as we learn God's laws and grow into His likeness we shall find our reward in this world in a life of usefulness and honor. To do this is to have found the kingdom of God, which is the kingdom of character and righteousness and peace.

CHAPTER VI

On Making Our Race Life Count in the Life of the Nation

N the Bible one finds over and over again the words "a peculiar people." Reference is made to the Jews as "a peculiar people,"—a people differing in thought and temperament and mode of life from others by whom they were surrounded. Now the race to which Americans of African lineage belong is often described as "a peculiar people," having had, as we know, a peculiar history. They differ in color and in appearance, and in a very large degree their temperament and thought differ from that of the people about them. Now the Jews because they were different from the peoples by whom they were surrounded, because of their peculiar religious bent, were able to give to the world the doctrine of the unity and Fatherhood of God, and Christianity, the finest flower of Jewry. It is then, I think, not too much to hope that the very qualities which make the Negro different from the peoples by whom he is surrounded will enable him, in the fulness of time, to make a peculiar contribution to the nation of which he forms a part.

What that contribution is to be no man can now tell, but we must keep in mind that the race is made of individuals and

"every man God made
Is different, has some deed to do,
Some work to work. Be undismayed.
Though thine be humble, do it, too."

As with an individual, so with a race. When you and I and all the other individuals that go to make up our race shall have learned to do well our own peculiar work, we shall be able to determine the bent of the race. It must fall upon you and me, who have had opportunity to work out in some measure our own individual problems, to give direction to the race. It is for us, therefore, to bring to the enrichment of our lives, as individuals, every quality which we are capable of cultivating.

There is in the New Testament a passage which I like to refer to and to think of; it reads something like this: "He that overcometh shall be clothed in white raiment." The expression "He that overcometh" occurs several times in the New Testament. I am anxious that the Tuskegee students shall get the idea firmly fixed in their minds that there are definite rewards coming to the individual or to the race that overcomes obstacles and succeeds in spite of seemingly insurmountable difficulties. The palms of victory are not for the race that merely complains and frets and rails. I do not mean to say that there is not a place for race loyalty and enthusiasm. There is a proper and vital place for protests against the wrongs that are inflicted without cause or reason. Every race, like every individual, should be swift to protest against injustice and wrongs, but no race must be content with mere protests. Every race must show to the world by tangible, visible, indisputable evidence that it can do more than merely call attention to the wrongs inflicted upon it. The reward of life is for those who choose the good where evil calls out on every hand. That reward is moral character. The more temptations resisted—the more difficult the struggle—the more robust the character. The wholly innocent person is much less praiseworthy than is he who has faced temptation and has come out of it unscarred. The virtues of foresight and thrift and frugality, brought bravely to the front, will bring large material possessions which if properly used will refine and enrich life.

I am constrained to refer once more to that "peculiar people," the Jews,—a race that has been handicapped in very much the same way as the colored people. Their opportunities have been limited in many directions. In Russia to-day they are in many cases debarred from schools and from entrance into the professions. And, notwithstanding the barriers in this country, one of the most noted banking firms in the United States is composed of Jews. Members of a despised race, they made up their minds that in spite of difficulties they would not stop to complain, but would compel recognition by making a real contribution to the country of which they formed a part. The Japanese race is a convincing example of the respect which the world gives to a race that can put brains and commercial activity into the development of the resources of a country. What material difficulties the thrifty Hollanders have had to overcome in the development of their country! But the battle against water and wind has developed not only a country, but an energetic, thrifty people. The Netherlands have literally been made by these sturdy Hollanders, who because they overcame are looked upon as a great and happy people.

There is, then, opportunity for the colored people to enrich the material life of their adopted country by doing what their hands find to do, minor duties though they be, so well that nobody else of any race can do them better. This is the aim that the Tuskegee student should keep steadily before him. If he remembers that all service, however lowly, is true service, an important step will have been taken in the solution of what we term "the race problem."

For it must be remembered that no individual of any race can contribute to the solution of any general problem until he has first worked out his own peculiar problem. Some months ago I met a former schoolmate whom I had not seen for a number of years. I was naturally interested to hear about his progress, and began to question him. I asked him where he lived, and he said he had no abiding-place, in fact he had lived in a half dozen places since we parted. In answer to other questions, I found that he had no special trade, no special business, no bank account. I asked then what he had been doing in the intervening years, and he answered he had been travelling about over the country, doing his best to solve the race problem. That man should rather have been at work at the solution of his own individual problem. An individual circumstanced as he was could not solve anybody's problem. It is important to have one's own dooryard clean before calling attention to the imperfection in the neighbor's yard. Each Negro can put much into the life of his race by making his own individual life present a model in purity and patience, in industry and courage, in showing the world how to get strength out of difficulties. The late President Garfield once said that no person ever drowned, no matter how many times he was thrown overboard, who was worth saving, and that remark, with a few modifications, might be applied to a race. No race is ever lost that is worth saving, and no race need be lost that wants to save itself. The world is full of little people who through lack of wisdom and patience and perseverance merely add to the world's burdens. The despised Negro has the chance to show to the world that charity which suffereth long and is kind and which never faileth. In the face of discouragements and difficulties the Negro must ever remember that nobody can degrade him. Nobody can degrade a big race or a big man. No one can degrade a single member of any race. The individual himself is the only one who can inflict that punishment. Frederick Douglass was on one occasion compelled to ride for several hours in a portion of a freight car. A friend went into the freight car to console him and said to him that he hated to see a man of his intelligence in so humiliating a position. "I am ashamed that they have thus degraded you." But Douglass, straightening himself up in his seat, looked the friend in the face and said, "They cannot degrade Frederick Douglass." And so they cannot degrade a single individual who does not want to be degraded. Injustice cannot work harm upon the oppressed without injuring the oppressor. The Negro people must live the precepts taught by the Christ. They must go on multiplying, day by day, deeds of worthiness, piling them up mountain high. And just as you and I, as individuals, are called upon to serve the race of which we are a part, so let us as a race recognize the fact that we are a part of a great nation which we are bound to serve.

www.ingramcontent.com/pod-product-compliance
Lightning Source LLC
Chambersburg PA
CBHW071449040426
42445CB00012BA/1493